mini bumper
b o o k   o f

Jazz *and* BLUES

Production: Sadie Cook
Cover design and typesetting by PCD

Published 1997

All Of Me

Words and Music by
SEYMOUR SIMONS and GERALD MARKS

Lyrics:

You took my kiss-es and you took my love,___ you taught me how to care,

You took my glad-ness when you went a-way,___ my star of hope is

am I to be____ just the rem-nant of____ a

all that re-mains___ is a me-mo-ry____ that

April In Paris

Words by E Y HARBURG
Music by VERNON DUKE

A-pril's in the air, but here in Pa - ris, A - pril wears a dif - ferent gown.

You can see her waltz - ing down the street, the tang of

Avalon

Words by AL JOLSON and B G DE SYLVA
Music by VINCENT ROSE

Ev - 'ry morn - ing mem -'ries
Just be - fore I sailed a -

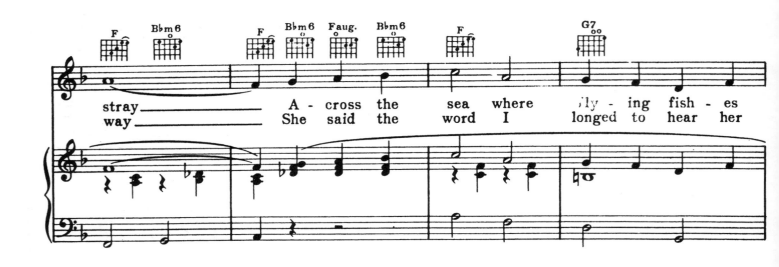

stray_____ A - cross the sea where fly - ing fish - es
way_____ She said the word I longed to hear her

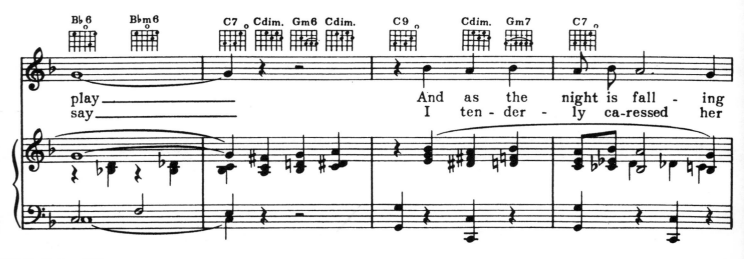

play_____ And as the night is fall - ing
say_____ I ten - der - ly ca-ressed her

Birdland

Words by JON HENDRICKS
Music by JOSEF ZAWINUL

(Solo Scat Sing ad lib during Repeat and fade)

Pay the gate, don't be late. It's a date. Whatlay' know.
If y' dig, then you'll dig it's a groove. Quite a groove,
'Cause y' t' move. Come in twos, pay your dues. What can you lose?
Just your blues! So lose them! The band swingin' one and all and
what a ball! Yeah! Music is good, music is better than good. Pretty good,
very nice, really very good. Things are being like they should. Very good,
very good, very good. All y' gotta do is lend an ear an' listen to it.
Then you dig a little sooner than soon. You'll be diggin'
everything – diggin' all the music. What a ball!
How y' gonna figure out a way t' bring it all about amid a
lot o' other music on the set'n on the scene, know what I mean?
How y' gonna separate the music from the scene?
Gonna have t' keep the memory clean. Y' gonna hear
a lotta' sound-- a lotta soun'. . .

Bewitched

Words by LORENZ HART
Music by RICHARD RODGERS

Moderato

He's a fool and don't I know it, But a fool can have his charms;

I'm in love and don't I show it, Like a babe in arms.

Body And Soul

Words by ROBERT SOUR,
EDWARD HEYMAN and FRANK EYTON
Music by JOHNNY GREEN

But Not For Me

Music and Lyrics by
GEORGE GERSHWIN and IRA GERSHWIN

The Birth Of The Blues

Words by B G De SYLVA and LEW BROWN
Music by RAY HENDERSON

C Jam Blues

By DUKE ELLINGTON

The Dixieland Ball

Words by BUDDY KAYE
Music by AL FRISCH

With A Dixieland Beat

Chorus — Get a new shine on your shoes, We're gon-na shim-sham-shim-my to the blues, To-night's the big night for THE DIX-IE-LAND BALL.

We'll rub el-bows with the swells, The sug-ar dad-dys and their styl-ish belles, So let's start head-in' for THE DIX-IE-LAND BALL.

★Symbols for Guitar, Diagrams for Ukulele

Come Rain Or Come Shine

Words by JOHNNY MERCER
Music by HAROLD ARLEN

Crazy Rhythm

Words by IRVING CAESAR
Music by JOSEPH MEYER and
ROGER WOLFE KAHN

REFRAIN

Cry Me A River

Words and Music by
ARTHUR HAMILTON

Don't Get Around Much Any More

Words by BOB RUSSELL
Music by DUKE ELLINGTON

Fever

Words and Music
JOHN DAVENPORT and EDDIE COOL

1. Nev-er know how much I love you, Nev-er know how much I
2. Sun lights up the day-time, Moon lights up the

care. When you put your arms a-round me, I get a
night. I light up when you call my name, And you

fe-ver that's so hard to bear.)
know I'm gon-na treat you right.} You give me fe-ver

Verse 3 Romeo loved Juliet
Juliet she felt the same,
When he put his arms around her, he said,
"Julie, baby you're my flame."

Chorus Thou givest fever, when we kisset
Fever with my flaming youth,
Fever – I'm afire
Fever, yea I burn forsooth.

Verse 4 Captain Smith and Pocahantas
Had a very mad affair,
When her Daddy tried to kill him, she said,
"Daddy-o don't you dare."

Chorus Give me fever, with his kisses,
Fever when he holds me tight.
Fever – I'm his Missus
Oh Daddy won't you treat him right.

Verse 5 Now you've listened to my story
Here's the point that I have made:
Chicks were born to give you fever
Be it fahrenheit or centigrade.

Chorus They give you fever when you kiss them,
Fever if you live and learn.
Fever – till you sizzle
What a lovely way to burn.

Fly Me To The Moon

Words and Music by
BART HOWARD

54

A Foggy Day

Music and Lyrics
GEORGE GERSHWIN and IRA GERSHW[IN]

© 1937 (renewed) Chappell & Co Inc, USA
Warner/Chappell Music Ltd, London W1Y 3FA

The Girl From Ipañema (Garota De Ipañema)

Original Words by VINICIUS DE MORAES
English Words by NORMAN GIMBEL
Music by ANTONIO CARLOS JOBIM

Guess I'll Hang My Tears Out To Dry

Words by SAMMY CAHN
Music by JULE STYNE

Very broad

Cm7/A♭   Bm7/A♭   B♭m7/A♭   E♭+5/A♭   A♭maj7   Fm7/A♭

Some-bod-y said just for-get a-bout him, so I gave that treat - ment a

Cm7   E♭7/6   E♭7+5   A♭13   A♭13-9   D♭maj7   G♭7-5 G♭7

try; Strange - ly e-nough I got a-long with-out him,

A♭   Fm7   Dm9-5   G7-9   Cm7   Cm7/F   F7-9

then one day he passed me right by, oh well, I

Freely

B♭m7   A♭   G/A♭   G♭/A♭   A/A♭   E♭7   A♭

guess I'll hang my tears out to dry._____

Here's That Rainy Day

Words by JOHNNY BURKE
Music by JAMES VAN HEUSEN

I Don't Stand A Ghost Of A Chance

Words by BING CROSBY
and NED WASHINGTON
Music by VICTOR YOUNG

68

How High The Moon

Words by NANCY HAMILTON
Music by MORGAN LEWIS

I've Got A Crush On You

Music and Lyrics by
GEORGE GERSHWIN and IRA GERSHWIN

It Don't Mean A Thing (If It Ain't Got That Swing)

Words by IRVING MILLS
Music by DUKE ELLINGTON

It's All Right With Me

Words and Music by
COLE PORTER

in the wrong style ___ tho' your smile is love-ly, it's the wrong smile, ___

it's not {her}{his} smile ___ but such a love-ly smile ___ that It's All Right

With Me. ___ You can't know how hap-py I am that we

met, I'm strange-ly at-tract-ed to you, ___ There's some-one I'm

try-ing so hard to for-get. Don't you want to for-get some-one too? ___

Jeepers Creepers

Words by JOHNNY MERCER
Music by HARRY WARREN

wea-ther vane points to gloom-y, It's got-ta be sun-ny
road to com plete dis - as - ter? Each new day I'm fall - in'

F7   Bb   Dm   A7

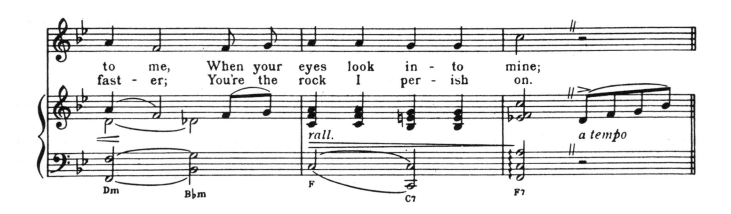

to me, When your eyes look in - to mine;
fast - er; You're the rock I per - ish on.

Dm   Bbm   F   C7   F7

rall.   a tempo

CHORUS

Jeep-ers Creep-ers! Where'd ya get those peep-ers? Jeep-ers Creep-ers!

mf (with a swing)

Dm F7 Dm7 Bb   F7   F9 F7 Bb   Dm F7 Dm7 Bb

Where'd ya get those eyes? Gosh all git up! How'd they get so lit up?

F7 F9 F7 Bb   Dm F7 Dm7 Bb   F7 F9 F7 Bb9 Bb
                                                    add Bb

It's Only A Paper Moon

Words by BILLY ROSE
and E Y HARBURG
Music by HAROLD ARLEN

The Lady Is A Tramp

Words by LORENZ HART
Music by RICHARD RODGERS

Won't dish the dirt with the rest of the girls, _____ That's why the la-dy is a tramp. _____ I like the free fresh wind in my hair, _____ Life with-out care. _____ I'm broke, _____ it's oke, _____

Laura

Words by JOHNNY MERCER
Music by DAVID RAKSIN

seem, _____ she gave _____ your ve - ry first

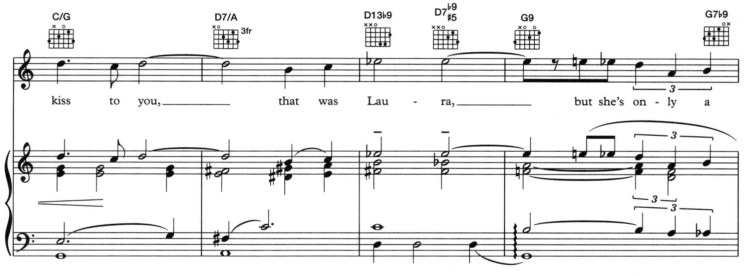

kiss to you, _____ that was Lau - ra, _____ but she's on - ly a

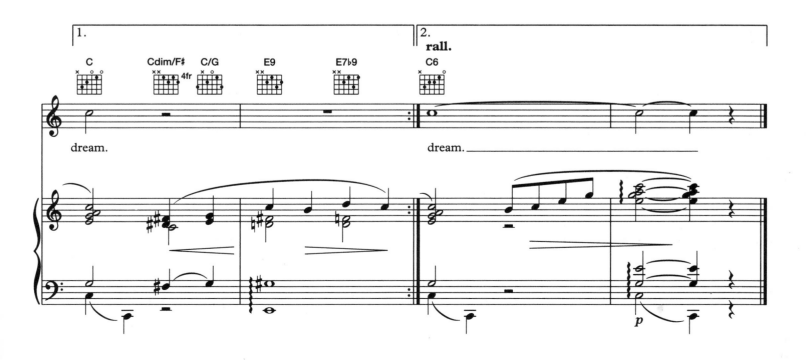

dream.   dream. _____

Let There Be Love

Words by IAN GRANT
Music by LIONEL RAND

Manhattan

Words by LORENZ HART
Music by RICHARD RODGERS

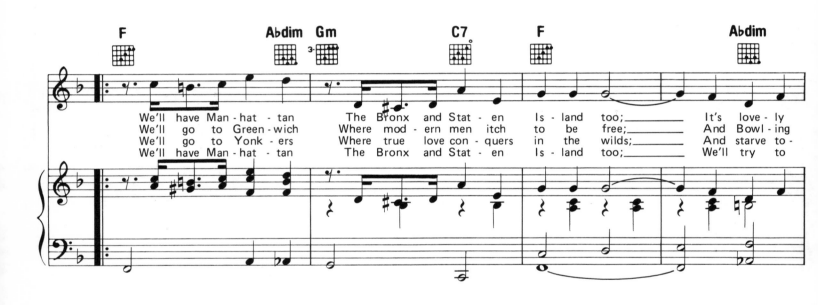

We'll have Man-hat-tan   The Bronx and Stat-en   Is-land too;_____   It's love-ly
We'll go to Green-wich   Where mod-ern men itch   to be free;_____   And Bowl-ing
We'll go to Yonk-ers   Where true love con-quers   in the wilds;_____   And starve to-
We'll have Man-hat-tan   The Bronx and Stat-en   Is-land too;_____   We'll try to

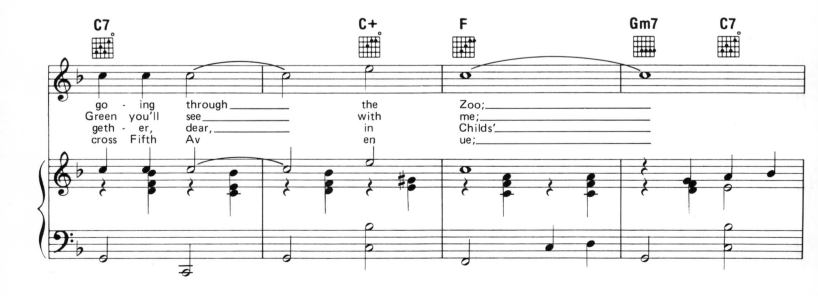

go - ing   through_____   the   Zoo;_____
Green you'll   see_____   with   me;_____
geth - er,   dear,_____   in   Childs'_____
cross Fifth   Av   en   ue;_____

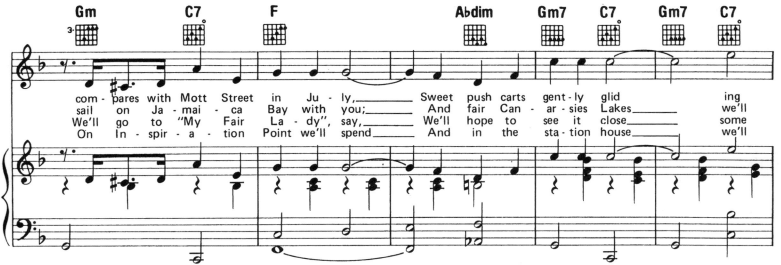

Misty

Words by JOHNNY BURKE
Music by ERROLL GARNER

thou-sand vi - o - lins be-gin to play, Or it might be the sound of your hel - lo, That

mu - sic I hear,___ I get mist - y, the mo - ment you're near.

You can say that you're lead - ing me on,_____ But it's just what I

want you to do,___ Don't you no - tice how hope - less - ly I'm lost,___

Mood Indigo

Words and Music by DUKE ELLINGTON,
IRVING MILLS and ALBANY BIGARD

One Note Samba (Samba De Una Nota So)

Words by NEWTON MENDONCA
Music by ANTONIO CARLOS JOBIM

Lightly, with movement

My Baby Just Cares For Me

Words by GUS KAHN
Music by WALTER DONALDSON

My Funny Valentine

Words by LORENZ HART
Music by RICHARD RODGERS

Nice Work If You Can Get It

Music and Lyrics by
GEORGE GERSHWIN and IRA GERSHWIN

The man who on-ly lives for mak-ing mon-ey Lives a life that is-n't nec-es-sa-ri-ly sun-ny. Like-wise the man who works for fame, There's no guar-an-tee that time won't e-rase his name.

Night And Day

Words and Music by
COLE PORTER

On Green Dolphin Street

Words by NED WASHINGTON
Music by BRONISLAU KAPER

'Round Midnight

Words and Music by
COOTIE WILLIAMS and THELONIUS MONK

C B C B A G# E
F♯m7-9-5 B7-9+5 E7 E7-9+11 Am(addB) Am7/G
real - ly gets bad 'round mid - night. Mem-'ries al - ways start 'round
F♯m7-5 F9(addD) E7-9 Am sus4 sus2 D9
mid - night, 'round mid - night; have - n't got the heart to
Fm7sus4 B♭6 Em7 A7 Dm9 G7 G♯°7
3fr.
stand those mem - 'ries, when my heart is still with
Am7 D9(addB) F9 E9 A Bm7 A/C♯
4fr.
you and old mid - night knows it too. When some

Skylark

Words by JOHNNY MERCER
Music by HOAGY CARMICHAEL

Someone To Watch Over Me

Music and Lyrics by
GEORGE GERSHWIN and IRA GERSHWIN

Some Day My Prince Will Come

Words by LARRY MOREY
Music by FRANK CHURCHILL

Speak Low

Words by OGDEN NASH
Music by KURT WEILL

Spring Can Really Hang You Up The Most

Words by FRANCES LANDESMAN
Music by TOMMY WOLF

Lyrics:
Once I was a sen-ti-ment-al thing,
threw my heart a-way each spring.
Now a spring ro-mance has-n't got a chance,

Star Dust

Words by MITCHELL PARISH
Music by HOAGY CARMICHAEL

Stompin' At The Savoy

Words and Music by BENNY GOODMAN,
ANDY RAZAF, CHICK WEBB and EDGAR SAMPSON

Medium Swing Tempo

Sa - voy, ___ the home of sweet ro - mance; ___ Sa - voy, ___ it wins you at a glance; ___ Sa - voy, ___ gives hap-py feet a chance ___ to dance. ___ Your form ___ just like a cling - in' vine, ___ Your lips ___ so warm and sweet as wine, ___ Your cheek

Stormy Weather

Words by TED KOEHLER
Music by HAROLD ARLEN

Slow lament

Swingin' Shepherd Blues

Words by RHODA ROBERTS
and KEN JACOBSON
Music by MOE KOFFMAN

What Is This Thing Called Love?

Words and Music by
COLE PORTER

Printed in Great Britain by Hobbs the Printers Ltd, Totton, Hampshire 1/97